3/23   £2.50

A Vision of

C000200714

JAMES HARPUR

A Vision of Comets

To Monique & Ian ...
A brilliant week!
Totleigh, November 2004
Luv
James x

ANVIL PRESS POETRY

Published in 1993
by Anvil Press Poetry Ltd
69 King George Street London SE10 8PX

This book is published
with financial assistance from
The Arts Council

Designed by Anvil
Photoset in ITC New Baskerville,
printed and bound in England
by Morganprint Blackheath Ltd

ISBN 0 85646 257 8

A catalogue record for this book
is available from the British Library

ACKNOWLEDGEMENTS

Poems in this collection have previously been published
in the following periodicals/magazines: *Acumen, Agenda,
The Moorlands Review, Orbis, Outposts, Poetry Ireland Review,
Poetry Nottingham, Poetry Review, Poetry Wales, Prospice,
Resurgence* and *Ver Poets*; and in the following anthologies:
*The Gregory Awards 1983-84, The Gregory Awards 1985-86,
Lancaster Poetry Competition Winners* (1985), *The Least Thing*
(1989), *National Poetry Competition Prizewinners* (1979),
New Christian Poetry (1990), and *Voices in the Gallery* (1986).

*To my mother
and in memory of my father*

CONTENTS

LIBRARY LOVE

Your burning hair brushes the mahogany
As your head bobs over your open book,
Plato's *Symposium* as far as I can see
From upside down Greek and your serious look.
Then, when you reach the bottom of a page
And for a second glance up, it's a race
Against time to guess your name and age
From your evenly freckled Celtic face.
For days we've sat so near but never spoken,
Unwilling to invite the stares of the library staff,
But silence need not confound us – for what token
Of love can't eyes flash out like a heliograph?

Let us then be lovers only with our eyes,
Until if, as Aristophanes says, our two souls,
Seeking their opposites from equator to both poles,
Merge together with joyful surprise,
Then I will shout so loud as to quench all lovers
Whose tight passion this calm silence preserves.

RAINBOW AT COLLA, COUNTY CORK

There a bridge between two worlds was revealed,
A bloom of colours settling on the soft grain
Of thickened purple sky, deepening the sunlit field.

Into the neutral atoms of crystal rain
Violet, blue, red had been poured and in an arc
Swept across like a sash of Indian silk.

REVISED MYTH

The snake lay still, the essence
Of snake generations compressed
Into each atom of nerve and muscle;
Its oily green coils glistening
With the dryness of glazed paint.

The warm-blooded serene saint
Leant over and let drip drops of holy water
Until like a fork of lightning spasm
The snake, crucified, spat and spat
Back the gospel with hiss and venom,
Its blind tongue flickering foil-like,
Head and tail split from each other
By the great sackweight of solid flesh.
Unpeeling itself, it began to shudder,
Then rocketed through the bracken
That crackled like rain on a live rail.

Wherever he went, the snakes vanished:
He lobbed a cross,
They darted into foxholes.
He clicked his fingers,
They slipped between the cracks of gravestones.
He mouthed 'Abracadabra',
They melted into their own mirages.

But while the saint kicked off his sandals
The snakes chewed their way through thick earth,
And they met, and snake ate snake
Until just one serpent, sweating in its juices,
Its back crusted with the hills of Ireland,
Lay still.

And now it lies waiting,
Swelling under the thin skin
Of the New Testament,
Waiting for the saints on St Peter's
To drop off, one by one,

Like stand-up ducks at a rifle range.

THE VISITATION

As if the grass had got too cold,
The sheep all stopped their chewing
And lifted up their sooty visors
Towards the misty wintery sky.

I heard it then, an eerie noise,
A rising falling wiry sound –
As from a wobbling metal sheet –
And there, breaking from the toneless white,

Two swans, one close above the other,
Transformed from china ornaments,
Were thickening in the shape of swans
The otherwise invisible light.

In perfect beat the crafted wings
Like oar-blades crisply cut the air
Sustaining their angelic bodies
And direction-pointing necks.

It seemed there was a single swan
With its phantom hovering just above,
Both circling round the copper trees
Ready to drop down onto the pond.

With shadows sharpening on the grass,
They angled down and let their wings
Bloom up behind to break the speed,
And landed on the liquid glass,

Reposing on their white reflections,
Again two china ornaments.

THE SANDCASTLE FORM

He slices the sharp red spade
Into the virgin beige sand,
Scoops out a circle and smoothes
The moat with his grainy-furred hand.

He shovels up a mound of raw stuff
Until it's ready to be fashioned,
Then with a clout in the centre
The tip sinks, the base is fattened.

He carves out the walls, slaps on
Mush (after the portal cracked)
And to keep out seepage, tunnelling crabs,
He pats the foundations till compact.

Absorbed, intent, this master builder,
Unaware of the incoming tide,
Takes a lolly-stick and cuts out
Crenellations on every side.

He nicks off nodules and checks
That pearly pink shells are pressed
Right into the walls, then slots in
Seaweed on top, as the royal crest.

Suddenly his name is called from afar,
Breaking the spell of concentration.
With reluctance he walks away,
Glancing back at his doomed creation.

When the first wave reaches the castle
Multi-turreted, exact and trim,
He is too far away across the shore
To see it melt the castle's rim.

His structure now a creamy blob
As the waves sweep onwards, resigned
He sees it levelled on the shore, but
Intact and golden in his mind.

ROOK

Too high for any flood,
In a tree both bare and black,
A nest is lodged in a fork,
Growing daily though squalls shake
Each branch and batter the rook
Who flaps with tardy strokes
Back to his hide-out
Bristling like a stook.
He topples down groundwards
Till all his feathers flock
Upstream then slot in like slates.
The pumice-pale beak starts to poke
Away leaves, stilettoes the turf,
Then swaggering, braggadocio, he croaks
Out gall from the pit of his craw,
And listening, keenly as a crook,
Gathers his Sicilian shawl,
Plucks a twig, mounts and rocks
The breeze until he drops
Down into his secret nook,
Ready at once to carry on the work,
Incessant work, kept in the dark,
As when Noah, scenting the future,
Built his ark.

THE KINGFISHER

'*For most of us there is only the unattended*
Moment, the moment in and out of time...'
    – T. S. Eliot

I

A sudden flash of blue swerved swiftly
Away from my startled eyes.

II

As I was looking over a bridge
A bright small ball of blue flashed upstream.

III

One day at the stone bridge I looked
Down at the stream, when a bird
Zipped low-level and blue above the flow.

IV

By the stone bridge, being in no hurry,
I was watching pebbles ever-glassed by the water-gleam
When a shimmer of blue aquamarine
Zigzagged away upstream.

V

At the bridge past the church
Where I happened to pause,
I was absentmindedly caught up
In the clear chalk stream chuckling onwards
When I saw flashes of blue flitting
And dipping above the watercourse.'

VI

If I had to pinpoint the meaning
Of grace, I would cite the occasion
When I was casually leaning
Against a bridge of old grey stone,
Expecting nothing.
                                    Out of the blue,
The moment was redeemed
From mundane predictability
By a bird charged with such electric dye
That colour seemed to fuzz a fraction
Behind the plumage pulsing blue.

VII

After the blue bird had passed from view,
The clouds, no longer agape,
Returned to their usual blurry shape
And colours resumed a flatter hue.

VIII

When the kingfisher had shot
Into the future, I quickly forgot
How soon the quickened instance
Dulls back to secular existence.

IX

Unlike the ice-star Rigel, whose blue light
Burns light years from our sight,
This bird's colour pierced straight through
So both eye and bird seemed
To celebrate the burst of blue in between.

X

Down the long roll call that memory
Spindles up endlessly,
Among the welter of petty neuroses,
The grey events and faces,
A SPOT OF BLUE NOW STUNS THE MIND.

SWALLOWS IN MOTION

In the flush of an August evening
Swallows are nibbling the sky,
Squeaking like mice
In attenuated tremolo,
Swooping to the cropped level of the corn,
Then with a swing
Singing upwards to infinite skies.
Dipping and diving
They loop the loop,
Thread themselves through dissolving knots,
And then, as if their stalling hearts
Had cut out,
They plummet
And see the bristling fields crashing up
Towards their tiny craniums...
With flurry of wings
They re-engage the air,
Propel themselves up
Up to receding skies.
With needle tail-tips flickering,
They etch the evening with lines of light;
In convolutions of
Flowing calligraphy
They graciously curve the air,
Judder on a current
Then resume their rhythm
With a swing and a swish.
In dance chaotic,
They display random atomlike autonomy,
As if a vision
Of the microcosm
Had been granted in the dimming skies.

THE WINTER SWAN

for Eileen

The winter swan was furrowing the pond,
Drifting with the wind like an ice floe.
The feathers, nearly blue with utter whiteness,
Lay fanned together in the dormant wings
That were cupped and ribbed like scallop shells.
The long neck, pliant but braced with tendon,
From time to time would plunge the snowy head
With its tiger-painted china beak
Down to penetrate its own reflection:
The reflection penetrated by its down.

From the early descent of darkness
Snow loosened from the billowing clouds,
Swirling down into the silence of the pond,
And the swan ghosted through the flaky downpour,
Merging with the waft of white feathers
That were turning the world to pure perfection.
The swan relaxed the muscles of its neck,
Dropped it back into the valley of its wings,
And stopped moving beneath the settling snow,
The dark sky, the opened sky snowing swan.

GOLDEN FISH

Summer clouds stuffed with lassitude
Drop shadow down on this grey world,
On this water bordered by a muddy marsh
That tars the stalks of drooping sedge,
Where not even the aquamarine filament
Of a dragonfly can seem to implement
Its task to thrill the air and spin
Blue, over skims of green pond-skin.

Then as a flame concealed in a grate
Suddenly streams up in a rush of heat,
From under lily pads a live brand shot,
A glowing ember, a fish burning deep carrot
That flowed through the gloom propelled
By the copper fins of its rippling tail.
And now another from the same red hot mould
Followed the first. The two, snaking round
The ins and outs of murky tunnels,
Blazed out the blood-orange of sun cells
That had for years impaled their neutral skins,
Now fully charged to emanate, illumine
A trail through their Tartarean world.

In orbit round the outer edge they would
Vanish into darkness. But then like comets
Would return spurting back a track of flame,
Igniting the gluey depths of waterspace:
Would return as gods, golden, luminous,
Spreading glory through the surrounding mire,
Incarnated in bodies of frozen fire.

BREAKDOWN

In the garden, the moon was a tropical fruit.
I watched you swig down fortified wine
To wipe away the terrifying thought
Of the sun slowly rising, igniting London

To a jam of red buses, throttling taxis,
Tubular trains overripe and swollen,
Disgorging millions of maggot-white faces,
Each cocooned in layers of isolation.

Like dimwits we let you race around the house,
With your puffy red-veined eyes, slamming doors,
Blasting music on, drinking, smoking till the ash
Smeared your lips that babbled non-sequiturs.

Not one more morning were you able to cope
With whispers in the office, the giggles, the silence:
At 5 a.m. the doctor came, syringed you with sleep,
At 5 p.m. from the hospital, you rang us.

I still remember that night: lying in bed,
Listening to the doors bang – the music switched on
As if a poltergeist had been suddenly freed
And like a Fury was avenging our inaction.

Family, friends and work could not sustain you,
Drink and music could not provide an escape;
In your head, you had to bear your brain, to
Feel it coiled, eating its tail like a snake.

GERIATRIC WARD 18

The coloured patchwork of a television
Babbles away in a silent ward,
A giant toothless chameleon,
Pale as a pillow, reclines on a bed,
A black hole punched in his scaly skin.
Two eyes fix the ceiling unblinking.

In the room at the end, she's at death's door.
He is sitting at a table doing puzzles.
I say hello, smile and pull up a chair,
She blinks her drugged eyes and murmurs.
Tentatively, heart beating, I approach her bed
And articulate into her uncomprehending head.

A pallor from strips of neon radiation
Washes our faces. The central heating
Wilts the daffodils and carnations.
He tells me how she's been keeping:
Not bad on Wednesday, she had some fruit,
Not good on Thursday, she refused her soup.

I look at her bowed, sunken head
And fine wisps of silver flossy hair
From which erupts a hideous purple egg
Unconstrained by a thousand prayers.
He examines her fluid chart and in spidery ink
Records how much tea she has had to drink.

When she was first admitted, the evenings
Were failing, nights growing bitter,
Leaves turning gold, tourists were leaving.
Now the branches are blossomed with feathers
In avenues of wedding-dressed trees
Showering confetti with the lilt of a breeze.

She is curled like a claw clinging to life.
He is battling to stave off the horror
Of losing his beloved, for fifty years his wife.
The end must come soon now. The vicar
Has stuck 'The Lord is my Shepherd' on the wall
And a private payphone has been installed.

I say goodbye, kiss her, and back
Away while his stare pierces the glass pane.
His one eye tries to distract
Itself on what the window frames:
A Belisha beacon, a casual pedestrian,
A double-decker blotting out the sun.

HEALING LIGHT

In bed I count the roses on the ceiling,
    Rows and rows of paper bloom,
    A florescent rash that smothers the room,
And sends my sickened mind reeling.
As regular as fever the heating comes on
    Cranking with metal ache and quickly bakes
    Dry my moistureless hands and cheeks.
The clenched compress is warm as a scone.

Through bed-breath air I watch the evening light
    Close itself down upon the winter trees
    Forced upward, like chimney brushes, to freeze
Stiff under a star-peppered blue night.
Sapped and sweating, I wait for my hot brain
    To receive its nightly slop of dreams – then
    I see a brilliant moon, all of a sudden
New, and etched upon the brickle pane.

TITHE BARN AT BRADFORD ON AVON

The clouds had been sobbing all day,
Intermittent grizzling then tears streaming
Down in sudden outpourings of release.

By the time we got to Bradford on Avon,
The atmosphere had cleared up:
The clouds still mauve and bruised

But deepening the green of the spring grass,
The sun beginning to shaft clean holes of light
Through the grey disintegrating vapour.

Over the bridge, across the river,
The Saxon church huddled
Among the renovated period houses.

We walked past the 'Sufi Hall' –
Drawing rooms of Georgian elegance
Suffused with mystic Islam.

Behind and apart we saw the tithe barn,
Its myriad bricks like the tarnished scales
Of a fabulous mediaeval monster.

Entering, we felt the blackness pour down
From above the beams, thick as tree trunks.
Empty of golden sheaves, it smelled of mud.

At the west end, branded through the wall,
A cross of light, radiant with the sun,
Burnt into the soft black earth

The shining cruciform outline of itself
And poured, like molten silver,
Liquid light into the sodden mould.

HEAVENLY BODIES

The branches in this forest of yews
Had been forced sideways to breathe light,
Branches over branches, branches stifling branches.

The ever-shadowed ground was clear of grass
Except where a crack had let a blade of light
Cultivate a small green patch of moss.

A squirrel chattered its nails up a trunk,
Then silence from the dark groaning faces
That the trees had twisted out of their barks.

We walked in silence, not quite side by side,
A silence born from deadness of spirits
That once we had bitterly tried to unite.

In graveyards, yew tree roots, it is said,
Extend inch by inch like tentacles
And break into the skull mouths of the dead.

Something also had taken root inside us
So that thoughts that needed to be spoken
Were strangled by self-consciousness.

Sudden autumn sunlight outside the forest
Streamed into our dazzled blinking – and fields
Undulated, unencumbered of their harvests.

A line of beeches had been stripped of copper
Which lay in heaps and through which we shuffled,
Relieved to be in the crisp windless air.

Far off we heard the sound of a dragon roaring
Then saw a white balloon filled to lightness
By fire of torch, buoyant and soaring,

And there, too, an early moon, its masked light
Glowing softly like a Chinese lantern
Reflecting red sun in a pool of white.

Two heavenly bodies in unison!
Resisting gravity's pressure,
Pale globes on the deepening blue horizon.

HERACLEION

Above the stew of hot olive oil
I look out from a balcony.
A gentle breeze ruffles the Aegean
That spreads into folds, sighs, settles down
To rock the city asleep with its unrushed rhythm.

All points of the compass can be seen.
In front, a darker shade of navy marks the line
Where the ocean mirrors the bottomless sky,
And galaxies swim on and on
Like shoals of silver fish.

There, far to the west,
Halfway up the mountainside,
Village lights, clustering like the Pleiades,
Commemorate the horror of volcanic destruction
As candles lit in the window of the earth.

To the east, beyond the dressing-room lights
That stud the airport tarmac,
The horizon has been unzipped
And with its cord cut
The moon has floated up to glass the set sun.

The colour of old parchment, it freshens to lemon
And rising to familiar neon
It spots the Venetian gold – the old harbour walls,
Flaunting, like the clay disk from Phaistos,
Hieroglyphs of another world.

Back down below, the roof-tops slope off
And darken away from the city centre;

And a ship slides off quietly
To Santorini, Rhodes or Alexandria.
Panta rhei, everything flows, everything flows...

EOS

I awoke suddenly in darkness,
Saw time angled in ultra green,
Winced at the bulb that broke into beam,
Stuffed legs into trousers,

And felt the rail up four flights
To the roof and saw the horizon
Stretched low across the Aegean,
In great bands of ruddy light.

The sky was thickened by a grainy mist
But rose to a clear copper glow
Until night in deepening blue shadow
Arched its back over to the west.

A silent world was opening before me:
Above, the half-moon, as whole as Yin and Yang,
Smoked away in dry ice as it began
Its dawn dissolving into obscurity.

And now the flames burning red as Mars
Turned amber till more sky was lit
Rising higher to wipe clean bit by bit
The palimpsest of uncharted stars.

I waited for the sunball itself to fire the air
As it did in the beginning of time,
Illuminating swamps, benighted slime.
Then with a flash I felt my pupils flare

As the simmering rim of gory
Colour curved up through the gauzy vapours,
Then more tremulous blood-orange arose,
And more and more, flooding the eye with glory.

CRETAN EASTER

1 GOOD FRIDAY NIGHT

Just like lost souls shuffling towards Charon,
The silent black cortège follows the priest.
Their downcast faces manifestly mourn
The Spirit's descent into darkest night,
Demon-haunted regions of the deceased,
Flamed by fires devoid of any light.

A pagan spirit surrounds this grave procession:
Ranks of pumpkin-glow and chanting, incense
Inspissate the air with superstition...
And candle-sellers, camp-followers in beat
To a drum, trail as if in somnolence
The gaudy mock coffin, swaying up the street.
    His death so painted by the Orthodox,
    Perhaps he will rise like a Jack-in-the-box?

2 SATURDAY NIGHT

We fill the floodlit cathedral square
And listen to the microphoned transmission
Of the Mass that electrifies the air:
'Christ Jesus came to save us who have sinned',
But we heed only local tradition –
Devil's luck if our candles are snuffed by wind.

The approach to midnight heightens tension,
Priestly voices reach a higher pitch,
As the great clock hands reach their ascension
The world goes mad and giant bells ring out

Throughout the city, shooting fireworks stitch
The night with stars and raise the joyful shout
    '*Alēthos aneste!*' – 'He has risen indeed!'
    As have the winds that blow their ancient creed.

3 SUNDAY AFTERNOON

The country flowers are bright and fresh today,
The smell of charcoal rises from the fire,
In these hills we are blissfully away
From Golgotha and the Crucifixion,
Whose darkness is dispelled by the sapphire
Of the sea flinted white far off by the sun.

Our luxuriating senses prey
On the green grass and pollen-searching bees,
Olive branches that shimmer as they sway,
All empathising with the Resurrection.
But there comes just one moment of unease:
With Nature's heady intoxication,
    This spitted goat and bottles of black wine,
    Is Christ or Dionysus the Divine?

A REPRODUCTION OF CONSTABLE'S 'SALISBURY CATHEDRAL' IN A ROOM ON A GREEK ISLAND

For a moment, time and motion stop still:
Shadows are lengthening across the meadow,
Evensong voices collect together and fling
Jerusalem into the vast cathedral space;
An English summer evening is coming to a close.

Beyond the slit window, the wall
Extends to beat off the scorch.
Flies dizzy the naked light bulb;
One dives too low and a hand flicks out
With the autonomy of a donkey's tail.

At the wood-dark water of the stream
Emerging half-highlighted in the shade,
A cow, her burnished anvil-boned backside
Anchored on the bank, has raised her head
And lets water drool out of her mouth.

Here, airless heat dries the skin.
Whitewash thinly bruises the plaster,
Nylon mesh curtains are strung up
Like chickens in ragged weightlessness.
Drawers are parched with yellow newspaper.

On the path, a man with a hat and frock coat
Points his cane. His idle remarks are unanswered
By the bonneted lady, draped in scarlet,
Standing out from the greeny golden cascade
Of foliage like a bird of paradise.

There is dust under the jammed tap.
A cracked glass is flaked with toothpaste;
A cockroach glistens black in the corner,
The air is as hot as exhaled breath,
The bare walls are closing in.

Through the arching elms, towards the clouds,
The cathedral rises. The service is ending –
I shall not cease from mental fight –
While the light settles on the mitre-shaped windows,
The stony buttresses preserving stability.

What great lodestone must exist to draw up
This great spire and the smaller ones frosted on
Like stalagmites, and uplift the spirit
From the despondent, earthbound body
Into the coolness of England's green and pleasant land.

THE SQUID

With heat rising glassily from the littered sand,
Distant beach noises, grit-in-the-eye grizzling,
Fat Marias whaled high and dry and slumbering
Under the umbrella umbra, from the sea's edge
A man arose, spear-gun in one hand, while the other
Was disfigured by a clammy lump
Gripping the skin with blubbery feelers.
It was as grey as charcoal, bunkered as the moon,
An alien thing, sea-blind, that had closed
Coldly on human warmth in a deathly world.

Underwater world   has no sound
          only colours.
Towards the shore   waves break
          the sunlight
Into dancing lines   of spinning thread
          spun from gold.
In silence   in parachuting
          movements
Sea plants sway   in skirts
          borne upwards.
Tiger-striped fish   sail in tiny
          glowing shoals;
Out of rocks   a squid billows up
          pulsating
With liquid tentacles   that stream back
          in the slipstream.
Every fraction   of its shredded form,
          shivering with nerves,
Seems calm to the frogman   pointing his harpoon.

He now picks it off, amused at the onlookers
Who shrink from the white jelly-sack
That blobs about, the unspinal slop of suckered flesh
That dangles oilily from his hand.
Snatched from a sub-world of lungless monsters,
It is now flung down upon a stone again and again
For yet more pulp to be slapped into it,
Then hung to crinkle in the sun like a starfish,
Its ugliness dispersed by the grilling heat,
But its beauty still in depths to be found,
Pulsing over anemones.

TEFELI, CRETE

More like a warehouse than a café:
Old crates are stacked up,
And several sacks of raisins, roped,
With broken chairs on top,
Fill the dusty shadows of half the room.

The stone floor is littered with pips,
Butt-ends stamped like beetles;
The throbbing hum of the giant fridge
Packed with tins, cheeses, rudimentary sausage,
Is absorbed by farmers unwinding slowly.

The proceedings are iced by two neon strips.
The hazy grey-blue of the television
Stares coldly at the cross-eyed village idiot
Who fails with giggling blandishments
To unfreeze their electric conversation.

All faces are sun-glazed.
Only their big brown fingers move
To pick up doll's house coffee cups,
Tap cigarettes as elegant as chalk sticks
Or thrust down backgammon chips with a 'tchimp'.

Three, sitting in the corner,
Dirty vests glinted by gold Byzantine crosses,
Digest their cards, glance up,
Surreptitiously smiling with slyness of bluff,
Then chuck in their hands to start a new game.

A tiny girl drags a teddy bear by a string
Past a man too old for the fields;
His body has shrunk since the days of war,
But he still wears the black meshed headscarf:
Death remembered serves for death approaching.

No word is spoken here. Aches begin to ease,
Insistent tractor engine diminishes from the ear.
Now there are lion yawns, soon beds,
Then again waking in the blue-washed morning
To the brute rhythms of Hesiod's calendar.

ROMAN SOLDIERS AT VAI, CRETE

They carry their helmets and the white sand
Shifts as their feet crush out powdery tracks.
The sky is blasted white by the sun,
But the sea is fresh, the afternoon has begun.
They stop, unhinge armour and lie on their backs,
Moulding themselves into the softness of the strand.

A world away the Tiber is sluggish with slime,
Dead cats jaw the tugging river currents,
Rome is dissolving, her power long gone,
But in beatified memory the empire still lives on.
The stewing city intrigues have scant relevance
To these large Roman tortoises killing time.

Dark green fronds from the hearts of palm trees
Spray out, sway and caress the liquid air
Like sea anemones locked on the ocean floor,
And soothe away the sudden flashes of war
That haunts each brutalised soldier
Unable to enjoy a life of island ease.

They have no purpose here: they are slaves
To the luxury of undisturbed contemplation
That conjures up the shady courtyards of home.
Is it through strength or weakness that Rome
Can send these red-faced, leather-clad men
To guard against white-plumed barbarian waves?

SAILING FROM HERACLEION

The sun has sunk like an anchor in the sea,
The *Minos* bellows, snorts out plumes of smoke,
And slowly Crete begins to chug away
Till it's a glitter of gold lights in the dark.

The iron decks are spattered by the spume
Whipped up by winds that slam bank-safe doors.
The rudder blades churn the Aegean to foam
Infusing its black universe with stars.

Far out to sea, lightning seizes air and water,
A jagged streak of pink-magnesium
Sizzling from clouds secreted with thunder
That growls then crumbles on the horizon.

Inside, a half-awake, unshaven Greek
Shuffles zombie-like to snuff the TV out,
Then rejoins the ranks of bodies slumped asleep
In upright seats beneath strips of neon light.

In my dreams I see the Allies fleeing Crete –
The desperate race before dawn breaks
With Stukas dropping like crows from fading night
On soldier-gravid ships that sit like ducks.

But, at dawn, we'll be safe inside Piraeus
With cardboard cut-out hills backlit by the sun,
Its strange new amber light creeping over us,
As in an opera that has just begun.

AS THE NEW SPRING DAWNS

Virgil, GEORGICS I, 43–70

As the new spring dawns, ice melts
From mountains frosted white with snow,
And as a gentle wind blows from the west,
Clods of earth melt and crumble.
Now is the time for my bull to groan and snort
Over a plough slicing deep into the soil,
The ploughshare burnished bright by the furrow.
Only a field that has twice felt on its back
The summer sun and the strictures of winter frost
Answers the prayers of the anxious farmer:
His barns burst at the seams with the huge harvest.
But before we scar the plain with the plough's blade,
We should get to know the winds and the volatile weather,
The traditional tilling methods of an area,
And which crops will grow and which, still buried, will die.
Here corn will spring up and over there grapes.
In other places young trees and wild grass will thrive.
As you know, it is Mount Tmolus that sends us
Sweet-smelling saffron, and India ivory.
The effeminate Sabaeans send their frankincense,
The naked Chalybes their iron, Pontus pungent musk
From the beaver, and Epirus their prize-winning mares.
Nature fixed these everlasting laws in certain places
Right from when Deucalion hurled onto the empty earth
Rocks from which sprang a race of hard men.
And so to work! Let your powerful bull plough up
The rich soil in the first months of the year
So that the churned-up clods can dry
In the dusty heat of the full-bodied summer sun.
But if the earth is not rich, it will be enough

To plough it lightly with Arcturus in the night sky –
There, so that weeds do not stifle the budding crop;
Here, so there is sufficient moisture to stop
The fields from becoming arid desertland.

IN THE BARS

from the Greek of Cavafy

In the bars and brothels
of Beirut,
I gorge myself.
I didn't want to stay
in Alexandria.
Tamides chucked me,
went off with the Prefect's lad,
a villa on the Nile
and a palatial place in town
to boot.
I couldn't really stay on
in Alexandria.

In the bars and brothels
of Beirut
I gorge myself,
passing the time in an orgy
of mindless hedonism.
The only thing that keeps me going –
like something beautiful
that does not fade,
or perfume
that lingers on my skin –
is that for two whole years
the delicious Tamides
was mine, all mine;
and not for any house,
or villa on the Nile.

ORESTEIA

1 CLYTEMNESTRA AWAKES

She only lived to avenge that sacrifice,
And though she could not think of it or speak,
In dreaming sleep it burnt behind her eyes:
Just like a fish no longer gulping breath,
So her daughter lay, dead still, too weak
From struggling and waiting for her death.

Was it this nightmare of her child's pure blood
For over ten years clotting in her mind,
Or wild winds blasting her husband homeward
That made her squirm and mutter as she slept?
And when he strode ashore, battered, blind
To his own fate, the warning fires that leapt
    Across the mountains fired her rabid pain,
    The deadly circulation of her brain.

2 AGAMEMNON'S HOMECOMING

Every muscle of his back and arms
Had locked like bulbous roots from constant hate,
From incessant clanging of alarms.
Exhausted, numb and hiding his commotion,
He trundled stiffly through the Lion gate,
Through loose-haired women wailing their emotion.

Ten years his will had centred on one thought
That through those stricken days had borne
Him through and at nights when his sleep was fraught
With dreams of his daughter's immolation.

At last at home, he now would not be torn
From what had grown to be an obsession:
     A bath to cleanse his bloody, blackened life,
     A long hot bath... a massage from his wife.

3 IPHIGENEIA AT AULIS

In dusty windless heat, I soon shall die.
On smooth white marble, lying on my back,
I feel myself relax, dissolve beneath the sky.
The pollen-soaked air, the warm sun both promote
Easing of muscle, sinew that now seems so slack.
Before my eyes events begin to float...

I see my father rising from his bath,
Half in, half out – entangled in a net!
Struggling and struggling... then a woman's laugh,
A flashing blade – I see my mother's eyes
Transfixed by her son's ghostly silhouette,
Her pleas for mercy turning into cries!
     O Gods, preserve my father and my mother,
     Protect my sisters and my only brother.

MIDAS

Though cheated by phenomena like snow
That would deafen its white world then go,

And avenues of elms arching their leaves
But sickening to pulp from black disease,

It was only when the girl whom he adored
Said he was 'unromantic', made her bored,

That he took to pen and with its nib of gold
Inscribed on paper a permanent world.

Now he could coin in the bullion of words
A rising moon, an orchid, a flock of birds,

Or keep sunstruck snow crisp in couplets
And lovers lusty in freshly minted sonnets;

Could watch his mother in her death-bed agony,
His hot mind already stamping the obituary.

THE UNSENT LETTER
OF THE GASTARBEITER

'The autobahns look like runways.
The sleek BMWs have been taking off
to warmer weather down south.
Yesterday there was snow – the sky
filled with a million white petals.
Remember the police station at Antalya?
The calendar on the wall blossomed
with golden leaves, flowed with the Rhine...
(And that policeman who bellowed with
laughter when I asked if it was paradise!)
We have now got a new foreman.
His belly sags over his belt, he has no
eyebrows and goes red when he shouts –
but he is not too hard on us.
The 'economic miracle' does not extend
to my accommodation – I'm woken up by the daily
clearing of throats in the basin,
but your photograph shines out of the darkness,
a woman's tender look in the Fatherland.
I have shaved off my moustache –
you wouldn't recognise me now –
and silver has crept into my temples.
The women wear bright colours and look at us
with the contempt and fear of prison warders.
How are the boys? Tell them I saw
Hamburg play Eintracht Frankfurt
and I will try and send a football magazine soon.
There is talk of work at Essen – a pipeline.
Some have already gone there.
I will let you know what happens.
It is very cold now. I wear my sheepskin
in bed and listen to the radio stations.

I'm not sleeping well but the cough is better...
Anyway I couldn't take the time off.
Please do not worry about me,
God watches over us and the winter
will not last forever...'

MAGNOLIA

As if overnight a flock of gentle doves
Had filled the twisted vacant branches,
With the lifting of the river mist at dawn
The light was peeling the magnolia tree.
The waxy flesh of every bud was splitting
Into pale mauve, soft pink and white,
Opening to the fresh and early air
And everywhere upon the candelabra frame
The soft flamingo flames of flowers
Were rubinescing in the first red flow of sun.

ONE DAY IN SPRING

Night cleared
And the day arose unsullied,
An even ceramic blueness,
Pale and smooth as eggshell.
I lifted the heavy sash window,
Stood back and looked at what was framed:
The acacia's trunk was black and bare,
The branches dank and rilled
Like fingers left too long in water,
Twisting down from swollen joints
Tapering into fine capillaries.

In the gaps between
These winter-darkened gnarled bones
Space and water shone,
The River Thames flowed on towards the city,
The grain of its lush water
Stroked by the sun
Into swathes of tiny sparkling fires,
A mosaic of shifting diamond glitter
Igniting, guttering into patterns
Forming, dying with the onward flow.

The year was heating up.
The sun was higher in the sky,
Was burning into earth and water
Bringing brightness to the day,
And flashing as a distant brilliant star
To observers scanning the night sky
Light years away.

THE HAUNTING

I see you profiled in the window of a bus,
Or in a queue, your smile on someone else's face.

You are what might have been, a spirit from the past.
At night I hold you in my dreams and lay your ghost.

THE INVITATION

Today a letter comes out of the blue.
My name in your writing reminds me of when
The world hinged on a letter from you.
So why write now? Why all of a sudden?
The answer is a gilt-edged card
Announcing your wedding. I read his name
And know this time it's over. It'll be hard
To burn the memories – all the same
I'm sure my very dogged self's devotion
To duty will take control, and I may retire
From the limbo of long-dying emotion,
Inviting your invitation to the fire.

PRISONERS OF CONSCIENCE WINDOW, SALISBURY CATHEDRAL

Their disembodied heads float
Below the underwater blue
That flows from the glass mosaic.
Their eyes from which flies hope
Are raised high in helpless horror.
Their mouths hang agape in a silence
That caresses the air like a web.
If ever this glass did crack
And the blue shards dropped
Hissing like sheet ice,
What hot cries, frozen stiff
In their sealed throats,
Might bloody the air,
The outbursting outrage
Of those shattered by suffering,
By unadorned sickening despair.

In the centre, the Redeemer,
In whose agony the panes are steeped,
Is lit and relit on the cross
As daily the soft dawn seeps up
Into his brittle and broken body,
Thawing out the gagged cry,
Eli, Eli, lama sabachthani?
It rises, awakening other eyes
That had escaped in sleep
The glazed stare of those
Who would torture out submission
In the unholy cause of lies and fear.

But now at nightfall,
After a day of being fired to life,
They become once more extinguished
In the gloom of the lancet windows,
Consigned to cycles of light and dark
Till resurrected on the last day,
The blue membrane of glass
Rent like the veil of the Temple,
And the prisoners for truth coming forth
Blackened before the blazing sun.

EIN DEUTSCHES REQUIEM

He, a man of destiny, drives the rows of
Manic violins with his baton waving;
Streams of music fretted from bows of horse hair
Slice out the rhythm.

He becomes renewed with the booming chorus
Causing every pore of his skin to open
Up and breathe in flames of the activated
Spirit of Wotan.

Trumpet, cello, timpani join to rouse him.
Frenzied now he bangs down his fist with fury,
Jerks about as if he were in a silent
Black and white movie.

He enslaves the minds of his captive audience,
Has them eating out of his hand and then is
Driven to a goose-pimple climax, like the
Damning of Faustus.

Deep within the fire of his head, the doubts and
Fears are burnt. His mission is now before him –
Power surges into his heart, he strikes and
Seizes the moment.

Banners, cheering greet his emergence on an
Open railinged balcony. There before him
Stretch a million bloodthirsty torchlit faces
Chanting Teutonic.

TALLIS: *SPEM IN ALIUM*

The chandelier is icicled with glitter,
Frozen with loops of rainbow lace,
Lights the silent packed interior.

From the first of forty choristers
The purest notes rise into space.
With eyes shut you hear in the darkness

The heavenly spheres adorned with angels,
Spinning out music clear as glass,
Or light that bathes the lucent crystals.

Up the polychromatic sound soars
In sudden intense undulations,
Transporting us to beyond the stars,

Till at last the threads are all drawn tight
Into one glorious unification,
As spectral colours pour into white.

A HOME FOR RETIRED MINERS, ON THE WELSH COAST

The tissue of their lungs caressed the soot,
As, hunched in quasi-lunar dark and dust,
They cursed through echoes crunched out underfoot.
They'd wheeze and hack and rub their eyes to black
Then start again to chip away the crust,
Enlarging inch by inch their cul-de-sac.

But now they watch the ocean roll and roar
And taste the prickly wind that spikes their skin,
Feeling the freedom of the gulls that soar
Beyond the limits of width, depth and height,
As when the mind breaks through the walls within
And discovers rocks, gleaming golden bright.
    For these men, blind too long and cramped as moles,
    The sun relieves their dank and lunglike souls.

WELCOME TO CYMRU

The globule cats' eyes ignite and flash
Down the velvet tarmacadam of the motorway,
Stretched like tape towards the reddening west.

August stars are brilliant points
Above the heavy air that we speed through,
Dreaming in silence of a glowing destination.

At Port Talbot, the burnt machine smell
Penetrates and at the silhouetted steelworks
Lit by a thousand dotted fairy lights,

A lone chimney, rooted in Welsh earth,
Roars off fermenting liquid dragon-fire
Safely into the stillness of the night.

FIRE

In the beginning was Fire,
Barely moving across waters,
Sliding off a snake's back,
Hardly heating the earth.

Then a thaw of mountains,
Dinosaurs start to pick
The leaves off tree sprouts,
Nature warms to its task.

A flint, dashed, throws up
Cave huddle, silhouettes,
Macabre scene of dancing spears,
Blue agonies of bison.

A log starts from its fix,
Sends up a stream of sparks,
Is prodded in a flash,
And instinct smoulders on.

Gin curls up round ice,
Can penetrate the dumb,
The tumbler smoothes a face
Flushed and thirsting for fire.

Rosy-fingered Dawn strokes
The pallid world. The painter
Pallid with frustration
Reddens the white spirit.

The conductor tries to ignite
The kindling of creation:
The bellows are punctured,
Cold friction of violins.

The lover draws his verse
From a fire-petalled heart,
But syntax freezes the words
That are snuffed out like candles.

Martyrs stiff as pines
Bubbled up in resin stench,
Feed the living flames
That turn matter into spirit.

Fire within the Fire
Can quicken the living dead,
Can raise the spirit up
To the One, the Aten that is

Sun sealed in rushing flames,
Blazing in the outer heavens,
Shot through with Fire that is
Thunderflash and lightning bolt,

Lava glow, exploding shells
Shooting through the burning air –
That is the ether and core,
Reared up on the Sea of Galilee,

Was burning under Buddha's skirts,
The babbling scorch of Whitsun tongues
That consumes the paper, licking round
My fingers – FIRE! FIRE! FIRE!

MRS DU PONT AND HER
MANDALA GARDEN

Her bun of hair is as fine as spider's web
and as black as indelible ink.
As nature withdraws the moisture from her skin,
art fills in the cracks: from her cheeks
two red-stained sunsets bloom out
like imperial Japanese banners.
The faded elegance of another era
has receded behind her dribbling eyes,
the present encroaches like a cataract.

She drives an Estate limousine
though the Labrador for whom it was meant
is now an invisible presence –
the wind opening the door, footsteps on the stairs.
On the mantelpiece above the fireplace,
from which leap flames of golden bracken
and the turquoise scream of a peacock feather,
two Buddhas sit squat as brooding hens.
She can remember extricating them from the straw
of the crate that was shipped from Bangkok.

Three stories up, I can hear outside
the scrape and chink of a metal trowel.
From the window I see Mrs du Pont
kneeling on the terrace of her walled garden,
working on the octagonal flower bed.
In dimming autumnal light she turns over
the crusty soil, giving it a new dark bloom
among the miniature green and violet shrubs.
A clover-shaped bird bath is the central point
and sparrows peck its rusty water
while she flicks out worms away from the soil,
pressing down seeds that may not last the winter.

Age has shrunk her brain and time has become
scattered fragments that she speaks aloud;
disintegration is nearly now accomplished.
She pats and tightens the crumbly beds,
giving them form, order and symmetry,
nothing more to do now than to wait for spring,
and the colours to break from the octagon,
a mandala aflame with red, mauve and green.

SAMSON TO HIS MAKER

Lord, when with head shorn I was held down
And the ash-grey irons hissed like snakes
In the pulp of my eyes, would that they had burnt
Out the memories of the bodies
That fell below my arm as it bludgeoned, uncontrollably,
Anything soft and moving, the blood trickling
Like a nose-bleed from smiling mouths
Crumpling away into heaps fit for pig feed.
Yet even now the rabble heat my blood afresh
Chanting the letters of my name in the dustlight.
I know I must spill more blood
In one final act of vision, must quench the spirit
That smoulders behind the slippery pink screen
Of scar-blebbed skin masking the brazier of my head.
Now, when a breeze blows, I can feel
Curls of hair caress the top of my back,
And a thrill of strength runs up my spine
As I press, in half preparation, against these pillars,
Letting my muscles slither like rats under my skin.
Whether my shoulder bones, tightening and tightening
To a constrained pitch of sweat will suddenly
Buckle and lollop limply out of joint and hang
Like a woman's ungirdled breasts,
Or whether I can unlodge these spine-tight columns,
You, my Lord, beyond time, alone know.
Only this I pray: that if I dislocate the stones,
Let me quickly enter the dark night of death
Before my body breaks beneath the cascade of slabs,
And let me rise into your kingdom,
The blackness of my sins washed away by tears,
And grant that I may see the dawn hover in stillness

Over a river winding through the trees of a meadow
Whose grass falls softly beneath my feet
As I run towards the water's edge,
My eyes healed, blinded by your glory rising.

THE MAGI

Down in the desert,
Three camels clinked through sand
Shimmering like frost
From stretching dunes of stars
Which, as if a glass dome had shattered,
Were sprayed
Frozen still in their fall.

Three Persian pilgrims,
For three days drifting homewards,
One by one by one,
Linked by a silence come
From Bethlehem.
Amid the breath of cow and ox
Milking the straw-filled air,
Their brains chattering with hope
Were brought to silence
As a crisis cry for life
Broke from the mother's breast
And shivered their spinal cords.
Sheepishly they laid their gifts,
Glittering, rare and pungent,
Among the crusted stable opulence
And left, unable to conjure
A word of wisdom or wit.

Down in the desert,
Three camels clinked through sand
Shimmering like frost
From stretching dunes of stars,
Now fading like magic
Before the pastel, golden east
And the wakening red raw dawn
Yawning out its giant cry.

CHRIST AND THE WOMAN OF SAMARIA

I can remember it now:
The milky turquoise sky,
The pervasive summer heat,
The sheep sitting in the shade.

I meandered up the slope;
The stillness held every visible
Stone and shrub in place,
And far away in another valley
Came the gentle clonking of a cowbell
As it dangled in rhythm
With a warm animal body.

My life had become as empty as
The water-jug I was carrying,
As stale as the distant walled town,
With its gossip, sex and intrigues.
But the air was clear
And a stream was cleansing its pebbles.
My blue silk gown was absorbing warmth.

I didn't notice him at first.
He was sitting by the well,
Dressed in the colour of a faded rose,
Half obscured by the trunk of a tree.
He asked for water,
And though his lips were dry,
His eyes were moist
And creased into fine laughter lines
When he lifted his hand to reveal
A locust with all its parts insheathed,
And I gave a gasp
Nearly dropping the water I was handing him.

And when he spoke,
The words seemed to lodge themselves
Deep within the back of my head –
What I said in reply seemed silly quibbling
But he didn't interrupt,
He just looked inside me to the bitter
Shrivelled root within my breast.

'God is a spirit', he said, and drew
An arc with his finger around his head;
And I knew what he meant,
Knew I had lived this moment before,
As if the glowing elements of a forgotten dream
Were tumbling out into the waking world;
I told him that I knew the Christ would come
To impress upon him my belief.
He smiled, and it was then I realised
Who it was, who this strange man was:
I felt a sudden stirring and wrenching within
And then a tight tug in my stomach rising
As if water were being drawn
Right up inside the darkness of my body
Into the dazzling blue light.

MESSIAH

The wind shivered the olive trees
Into a shimmer of whispers,
And smears of muck proclaimed His coming
On all the whitewashed walls.
Jerusalem was ready.
We waited, as for centuries,
For the clouds to dim the sky
And gauze the sun to an opalescent moon;
And silent lightning crickling the horizon –
A crack and the sky shorn
With a gash of inflooding light,
Our ribs sucking in our lungs
And the flaming gold chariot blazing nearer,
Horses white and flinting out sparks,
Their ruby eyes flashing blood,
Tails ripping loose in the wind;
And the god of our hopes
At last quenching our ancient prayers,
Coming to save us in a glory of light
Softening in strata and cloaking
The diamond core of his body;
His features too far to be seen
Yet erupting behind our eyes,
His glowing flesh melting and reforming,
Our hearts bursting like trumpets,
Our ears spiralled deaf by the winds
Blowing our enemies off the earth...

When the rabbi waddled up the street
On a dung-discharging donkey,
Our hopes fell one by one
Like the palms dropping before him.
We slunk off and got drunk.

One of us was sick standing up.
Our blood frets.
I can't get to sleep
The pulse is pumping so loud in my brain.
Change is in the air.

I go to sleep counting dead Romans.

AT THE TEMPLE OF JERUSALEM

A bloated sun burns the desert world to rust,
Diminishing heat shimmers over dust,
Throats are granulated by the grit,
Flies glint on scabs of donkey shit;
Warm and goaty smells thickened with disease
Float through streets sealed off from any breeze.
Indoors, a dog drops out its lathered tongue
And acid words are breathed by stale lungs.

Next day, a billion fires cleanse the east,
It is the last day, the great day of the feast.
With barren minds the muttering plotting crowd
Stand stunned as they hear him cry aloud
Words simpler than they could possibly think,
Bottomless words from which they cannot shrink:

'If any man thirst, let him come unto me and drink.'

LINDOS, RHODES:
THE LANDING OF ST PAUL

He steps ashore; the sun is at its peak.
Was it chance or fate that brought him to this place?
What bastard patois would the natives speak?
What sacred words would the Holy Spirit
Cause to pour from his animated face?
What weighted stones would fly at him like spit?

Fresh water and meat were turning in the minds
Of his men, sunburnt, taciturn with a violence
Turned inward to the gut. At least the winds
Had blown themselves into a gentle breeze.
No man, no bird, no cricket broke the silence
As he gave thanks, palms open, on his knees.
    And still Rome, like a polar magnet,
        Was drawing him closer with every sunset.

LINDOS, RHODES:
A KNIGHT OF ST JOHN

The cragged acropolis above the town
Is edged by crenellations of the fort
That in the dropping sun turns russet brown.
Above, a hawk glitters like starry fire
Then plummets down but sees he must abort
His mission to kill, his moment to inspire.

Faulk de Greville of the Order of St John
Surveys the town, the deep mauve, rock-gashed sea,
And revels in the beauty of the kingdom
Of Rhodes where lemons, olives, the plump gourd
Feed the inner belly with a delicacy
Ripe for infidels, not servants of the Lord.
    The sun has set. Like a hawk his eye
    Glitters with power – he drops a sigh.

DR HALLEY COMPUTES THE COMET

Your disembodied wig watches
While your pale scanning eyes,
Accustomed to infinite space,
Stare at the microscopic figures
Squiggled like Hebrew on yellow paper.
The candle blooms a bud of fire.
Your lips, murmuring at the silence,
Are the only outward sign
Of the calculations circulating round
The circuit of your brain.
A sudden interruption could wipe out
The concentrated work of a day.

You look up and stare into space –
Something has lit within your mind...
Time recedes to 1682,
About to board a ship for France
You see the rose-reflected dust trail
Of a comet glittering across
The deep blue prairies of space.
That night it hangs in the blackened sea
And haunts your sleep like a ghost.

You pick up your quill with a flourish
And continue your letter to Newton:
I am more and more confirmed that
We have seen that Comett now three times
Since ye yeare 1531...

Round and round the calculations click.
Nothing disturbs the midnight silence.
1531, 1607, 1682 – not three comets but
The same one returning again and again.
The thought grips you like cramp.

In 1758, the sockets that have held
The delicate dilations of your eyes
Have been for 16 years packed with mud.
But at Christmas your prediction comes true:
As Germany hardens under a night frost,
A lone astronomer tunes his telescope
And picks up an unknown star – your comet
Plummeting to the sun,
Locked in the circuit of the solar system,
While your disembodied spirit watches
From the liberation of a star.

A VISION OF COMETS

The flight was delayed.
Outside, the night sky was clear,
And the land that had received the sun all day
Now slept in silence.
It could have been a Greek island
Or the new land of America.
He was returning home, for good, or for bad,
And the welter of accumulated memories
And friendships loomed up from the pit
Of his stomach in sudden queasy waves.
Time ticked on and passengers sat in rows
Under the flickerings of neon
Slowly numbing themselves to the worry
Of wondering when the flight would flash up.
Eventually, sunk in the midst of
Painful feelings of regret and loss,
A sense of peace overtook him,
An inner inexplicable assurance
That his journey home was right.
He felt suddenly at ease and, turning round,
Saw people rising as one from their seats,
Quickly assembling their luggage and moving
Towards the gate for their departure.
He went back against the flow to find his bags
And say goodbye to those who had been his intimates.
Strangely, as he approached the place he'd been,
He saw what seemed to be starry darkness –
As if the wall had melted away –
And people vanishing into the fringes of his eyes.

He somehow knew the young man who stood there.
It must have been outside for the darkness
Stretched all around sealing the horizons.

He approached the man, who pointed to the sky,
And there, igniting the dark in golden sprays,
Eight glowing comets moved softly through the night,
Slowly rising, turning, dipping, gliding
Like gilded dolphins hooping through the ocean blue.
Their tails, from which auras of sparkle
Would fizz and fade, were interwoven and moving
As if guided by an intelligence,
As if the comets were on kite strings controlled
By this young man as he moved his hands.
Then the comets began dissolving –
Yet their particles realigned and coalesced
Into luminous strokes with dots and squiggles –
And he realised they were giant words of Hebrew,
That they were telling him what his purpose was,
What his mission was on earth.

THE SHOOTING STAR

In summer he would gaze up at the darkness
With its trillion burning silver pores,
And where the giant constellations ranged
Like the skeletons of dinosaurs.

And when the skies fell sooner into space,
When the forests became brown overnight,
He would watch the world disintegrate in rain,
Migrant birds printed on the evening light.

When the snow lay sparkling on the ground
He would crack out tiny stars from flintstone
And watch the pine leap up in flames,
But unable to ignite his dumb expression.

Then one night, as darkness poured over him,
A shower of light sprayed across the skies
And a star, sparking signals up his spine,
Shot through his mind, and brought fire to his eyes.

FROM FISHGUARD TO ROSSLARE

At Fishguard harbour a drizzly mist was hung
Dripping from the iron railings of the iron hull
As onto the throbbing deck steamed-up cars were driving.
The ship began to move, black fumes were flung
From the funnel, the sea spuming up towards the gulls
Then rolling down like a whale suddenly diving.

Amid the dining room's tropical heating
The blue nun with yellow teeth and tertiary pube
Sprouting from the wrinkles of her chin,
Like a bit of the salad she was eating,
Was making me queasy with her chat, her food,
Her debate whether to buy whiskey or gin.

I faintly recalled the last time I came here:
Deserted beaches, the wild Atlantic roar,
Names like Crookhaven, Ballinclea and Tralee,
Georgian houses crumbling in the peat-smoke air
And haycocks doming fields with ripening straw.
But now would all be changed, changed utterly?

At last, on deck, Ireland came into sight.
Wind began to cleanse the greyness from the air
And pulled our hair back like straining grass.
The sun shafted great propeller blades of light
Onto the reflecting windows of Rosslare
And the whiskey sea aflame like cut glass.

CLIMBING CROAGH PATRICK

From the car park
Croagh Patrick rises,
Hooded by apparitions of mist,
Featherlight, drifting,
Sealing off the dark sharp apex.
The path, rutted like a river bed,
Crawls and winds up, disappears.
Cracked fresh from a plaster mould,
Saint Patrick guards the ascent,
The white icing of his body
Melts in the rain,
The green shamrock paint is chipped.
On the right, a stream gushes
Down, fed with the intense
Internal water of the mountain.
The invigorating hiss of waterspray
Purifies the softening air.
Sunshine breaks through
The wet flannel of mist
And flames on rocks and stones,
Littered in the mushed sand
Of the quarrylike path.
        Looking back, the car park
Has begun to shrink,
The empty cars in primary colours
Have become miniature toys.
The air is cooler.
Sweat feels cold, my shirt sticks
Like a wet sheet, but I am hot.
Step after step I pick my way
Over the rocks. The stream's rush
Is now separated by heather
And Croagh Patrick looms massive,

Its dark peak glimpsed between
Disintegrating wisps of cloud.
   An hour has gone.
Aloneness has cloaked me
With a sense of ease.
I have freedom of thought.
For a moment I am no longer
A receptacle for petty jealousies
Or incessant mindless chatter.
My smiling muscles have relaxed,
My forehead furrows smoothed out.
I climb higher and higher
Till now the car park is a
Bejewelled glitter of chrome.
Beyond, out in the sound,
The dolphin-skinned sea
Shivers as the wind
Wrinkles its surface
In sudden swathes of light,
Changing the rub of the grain,
Myriad scales shimmering across
The surface of darker water.
The floating islands,
Emerald stepping stones,
Gleam under silvered gold.
Shafts of light irradiate through,
The white mist floats
And seems to thicken and then,
In sudden patches, evanesce...
Before me the mercurial kingdom
Of water and mist dissolves!
Dark shadows cling to the sheer side
Of the mountain where the sun
Does not penetrate. Higher still I climb
And finally reach the ridge
Where I can see the other side

Of Ireland roaming away
In miles of soft turf.
Great stretches of peat fields
Lie cut away in brown strips,
The fibrous spongy peat
Knifed away clean like cake,
The cavities logged with water.
To the east, a concentration
Of steely blue vapours
Pours a swirling grey mizzle
Over the green brown land.
In perpetual movement, puffs of cloud
Buffeted along by the breeze
Sway towards the mountain.
    I rest before the final ascent
Where the track narrows
And angles steeply at 45 degrees.
I watch the mists closing in
And a father and son
Walk seven times round
One station of the Cross.
Climbers clamber past me
Towards the top of Croagh Patrick.
The sun is obliterated behind
The smothering grey wetness
That settles uncomfortably
Like insidious feelings
Coming home to haunt.
I cannot tell how steeply
The mountain drops away
In the pale monotonous light.
A voice tells me that having come
As far as I have come,
Not to reach to the top would be
An act to be regretted.
And yet the immaterial

Tunnel-walls of cold mist
Suddenly unnerve me.
Behind their frail drapings
Acres of light stretch away
To a horizon of hills.
My bouldered path narrows.
No ministering angels urge me on.
No voice of God.
There is no burning bush.
The wind shrills away
In sudden icy waves
In the warren of my ears,
Croagh Patrick, no different
From when its molten earth
Cooled at the start of time,
Rises above my aspirations.
I turn my back on the top.
Two pilgrims pass me and within
Fifteen yards I see them disappear
In underwater slow motion
Into the formless clouds,
Like ghosts into a snowstorm.

Tunnel-walls of cold mist.
Suddenly unnerve me.
Behind their frail drapings
Acres of light stretch away
To a horizon of hills.
My bouldered path narrows.
No ministering angels urge me on
No voice of God.
There is no burning bush.
The wind shuffs away
In sudden sea waves
In the warren of my ears.
Croagh Patrick, no different
From when its molten earth
Cooled at the start of time,
Rises above my aspirations.
I turn my back on the top.
Two pilgrims pass me and within
Fifteen yards I see them disappear
In underwater slow motion
Into the formless clouds,
Like ghosts into a snowstorm.